SOUTH CAROLINA CODE OF LAWS

TITLE 18
APPEALS

2020 EDITION

Revised on January 7, 2020
By West Hartford Legal Publishing

SOUTH CAROLINA LEGISLATURE

Table of Contents

CHAPTER 1 General Provisions — 5

CHAPTER 3   Appeals From Magistrates in Criminal Cases — 10

CHAPTER 7 Appeals to Circuit and County Courts in Other Cases — 13

  ARTICLE 1   General Provisions — 13

CHAPTER 9   Appeals to Supreme Court and Court of Appeals — 26

CHAPTER 1 General Provisions

SECTION 18-1-10. Title covers all appeals in civil and criminal actions; exceptions.

The only mode of reviewing a judgment or order in a civil or criminal action, other than the mode prescribed for particular matters in Titles 14, 15, and 17, shall be as prescribed by this title.

HISTORY: 1962 Code Section 7-1; 1952 Code Section 7-1; 1942 Code Section 771; 1932 Code Section 771; Civ. P. '22 Section 636; Civ. P. '12 Section 374; Civ. P. '02 Section 335; 1870 (14) 349; 1960 (51) 1750.

SECTION 18-1-20. Definitions.

As used in reference to courts and court procedure in this Title the following terms shall be interpreted as follows:

(1) The words "real property" and "real estate" are coextensive with lands, tenements and hereditaments.

(2) The words "personal property" include money, goods, chattels, things in action and evidences of debt.

(3) The word "property" includes real and personal property.

(4) The word "clerk" signifies the clerk of the court in which the action is pending and, in the Supreme Court or the court of appeals, the clerk of the county mentioned in the title of the complaint or in another county to which the court may have changed the place of trial, unless otherwise specified.

HISTORY: 1962 Code Section 7-16; 1952 Code Sections 7-16 to 7-19; 1942 Code Sections 897-900; 1932 Code Sections 897-900; Civ. P. '22 Sections 845-848; Civ. P. '12 Sections 482-485; Civ. P.

'02 Sections 444-447; 1870 (14) 466-469; 1960 (51) 1926; 1999 Act No. 55, Section 25, eff June 1, 1999.

SECTION 18-1-30. Who may appeal.

Any party aggrieved may appeal in the cases prescribed in this title.

HISTORY: 1962 Code Section 7-2; 1952 Code Section 7-2; 1942 Code Section 773; 1932 Code Section 773; Civ. P. '22 Section 638; Civ. P. '12 Section 376; Civ. P. '02 Section 337; 1870 (14) 351.

SECTION 18-1-40. Appeals by corporations in criminal cases.

In all criminal cases against corporations the right of appeal shall be preserved and the procedure therein shall be such as is now provided by law in other appeals in criminal cases.

HISTORY: 1962 Code Section 7-3; 1952 Code Section 7-3; 1942 Code Section 992; 1932 Code Section 992; Civ. C. '22 Section 4300; Civ. C. '12 Section 2833; 1911 (27) 41.

SECTION 18-1-70. Notice of appeal shall stay execution of sentence.

In criminal cases service of notice of appeal in accordance with law shall operate as a stay of the execution of the sentence until the appeal is finally disposed of.

HISTORY: 1962 Code Section 7-6; 1952 Code Section 7-6; 1942 Code Section 1031; 1932 Code Section 1031; Cr. P. '22 Section 121; Cr. C. '12 Section 100; Cr. C. '02 Section 73; R. S. 73; 1884 (18) 737; 1944 (43) 1256.

SECTION 18-1-80. Confinement until bail given.

Pending such appeal the defendant shall still remain in confinement until he give bail in such sum and with such sureties as to the court shall seem proper.

HISTORY: 1962 Code Section 7-7; 1952 Code Section 7-7; 1942 Code Section 1031; 1932 Code Section 1031; Cr. P. '22 Section 121; Cr. C. '12 Section 100; Cr. C. '02 Section 73; R. S. 73; 1884 (18) 737; 1944 (43) 1256.

SECTION 18-1-90. When bail may be allowed.

Bail may be allowed to the defendant in all cases in which the appeal is from the trial, conviction, or sentence for a criminal offense. However, bail is not allowed when the defendant has been sentenced to death, life imprisonment, or imprisonment for more than ten years.

HISTORY: 1962 Code Section 7-8; 1952 Code Section 7-8; 1942 Code Section 1031; 1932 Code Section 1031; Cr. P. '22 Section 121; Cr. C. '12 Section 100; Cr. C. '02 Section 73; R. S. 73; 1884 (18) 737; 1944 (43) 1256; 1996 Act No. 400, Section 1, eff June 4, 1996.

SECTION 18-1-100. Amendment to cure failure to perfect appeal.

When a party shall give, in good faith, notice of appeal from a judgment or order and shall omit, through mistake, to do any other act necessary to perfect the appeal or to stay proceedings the court may permit an amendment on such terms as may be just.

HISTORY: 1962 Code Section 7-9; 1952 Code Section 7-9; 1942 Code Section 775; 1932 Code Section 775; Civ. P. '22 Section 640;

Civ. P. '12 Section 378; Civ. P. '02 Section 339; 1870 (14) 353; 1878 (16) 698; 1880 (17) 368; 1912 (27) 625.

SECTION 18-1-120. How parties shall be designated on appeal.

The party appealing shall be known as the appellant and the adverse party as the respondent. But the title of the action shall not be changed in consequence of the appeal.

HISTORY: 1962 Code Section 7-11; 1952 Code Section 7-11; 1942 Code Section 774; 1932 Code Section 774; Civ. P. '22 Section 639; Civ. P. '12 Section 377; Civ. P. '02 Section 338; 1870 (14) 352.

SECTION 18-1-130. Review of intermediate orders affecting judgment.

Upon an appeal from a judgment the court may review any intermediate order involving the merits and necessarily affecting the judgment.

HISTORY: 1962 Code Section 7-12; 1952 Code Section 7-12; 1942 Code Section 777; 1932 Code Section 777; Civ. P. '22 Section 642; Civ. P. '12 Section 380; Civ. P. '02 Section 341; 1870 (14) 355.

SECTION 18-1-140. Judgment on appeal.

Upon an appeal from a judgment or order the appellate court may reverse, affirm or modify the judgment or order appealed from as to any or all of the parties and may, if necessary or proper, order a new trial. When the judgment is reversed or modified the appellate court may make complete restitution of all property and rights lost by the erroneous judgment.

HISTORY: 1962 Code Section 7-13; 1952 Code Section 7-13; 1942 Code Section 778; 1932 Code Section 778; Civ. P. '22 Section 643; Civ. P. '12 Section 381; Civ. P. '02 Section 342; 1870 (14) 356; 1960 (51) 1751.

SECTION 18-1-150. Certiorari to magistrates or municipal court.

Whenever a person shall have been convicted in a municipal court or a magistrates court such person shall have the right, upon petition, to obtain from any circuit judge or justice of the Supreme Court at chambers or in open court a writ of certiorari requiring such municipal court or magistrate to certify the entire record of the case together with a copy of the municipal ordinance or a reference to the statute involved, as the case may be, and including the rulings, findings and sentence, returnable at such time as such circuit judge or justice of the Supreme Court may direct, and upon the hearing of the writ such circuit judge or justice of the Supreme Court shall have the same jurisdiction of the entire matter as circuit judges now have in cases appealed from municipal courts or magistrates courts.

HISTORY: 1962 Code Section 7-14; 1952 Code Section 7-14; 1942 Code Section 994; 1932 Code Section 994; 1928 (35) 1317.

SECTION 18-1-160. Where undertakings must be filed.

The various undertakings required to be given by this title must be filed with the clerk of the court, unless the court expressly provides for a different disposition.

HISTORY: 1962 Code Section 7-15; 1952 Code Section 7-15; 1942 Code Section 824; 1932 Code Section 824; Civ. P. '22 Section 772; Civ. P. '12 Section 458; Civ. P. '02 Section 420; 1870 (14) 438.

SECTION 18-1-170. Rules of construction.

The rule of the common law that statutes in derogation of that law are to be strictly construed has no application to this title.

HISTORY: 1962 Code Section 7-20; 1952 Code Section 7-20; 1942 Code Section 902; 1932 Code Section 902; Civ. P. '22 Section 850; Civ. P. '12 Section 487; Civ. P. '02 Section 448; 1870 (14) 470.

CHAPTER 3   Appeals From Magistrates in Criminal Cases

SECTION 18-3-10. Appeals to Court of Common Pleas.

Every person convicted before a magistrate of any offense whatever and sentenced may appeal from the sentence to the Court of Common Pleas for the county.

HISTORY: 1962 Code Section 7-101; 1952 Code Section 7-101; 1942 Code Section 1024; 1932 Code Section 1024; Cr. P. '22 Section 144; Cr. C. '12 Section 93; Cr. C. '02 Section 66; G. S. 2646; R. S. 66; 1870 (14) 403; 1937 (40) 80; 1994 Act No. 520, Section 4, eff September 23, 1994.

SECTION 18-3-20. How appeals shall be taken and prosecuted.

All appeals from magistrates' courts in criminal causes shall be taken and prosecuted as prescribed in this chapter.

HISTORY: 1962 Code Section 7-102; 1952 Code Section 7-102; 1942 Code Section 1024; 1932 Code Section 1024; Cr. P. '22

Section 114; Cr. C. '12 Section 93; Cr. C. '02 Section 66; G. S. 2646; R. S. 66; 1870 (14) 403; 1937 (40) 80.

SECTION 18-3-30. Time for appeal and statement of grounds; payment of fine does not waive right of appeal.

(A) The appellant, within ten days after sentence, shall file notice of appeal with the clerk of circuit court and shall serve notice of appeal upon the magistrate who tried the case and upon the designated agent for the prosecuting agency or attorney who prosecuted the charge, stating the grounds upon which the appeal is founded.

(B) A person convicted in magistrates court who pays a fine assessed by the court does not waive his right of appeal and, upon proper notice, may appeal his conviction within the time allotted in this section.

HISTORY: 1962 Code Section 7-103; 1952 Code Section 7-103; 1942 Code Section 1025; 1932 Code Section 1025; Cr. P. '22 Section 115; Cr. C. '12 Section 94; Cr. C. '02 Section 67; 1880 (17) 493; 1968 (55) 2309; 1973 (58) 359; 2010 Act No. 269, Section 1, eff June 24, 2010.

SECTION 18-3-40. Papers shall be filed with clerk of court.

Within ten days after service the magistrate shall file the notice in the office of the clerk of court, together with the record, a statement of all the proceedings in the case, and the testimony taken at the trial as provided in Section 22-3-790.

HISTORY: 1962 Code Section 7-104; 1952 Code Section 7-104; 1942 Code Section 1026; 1932 Code Section 1026; Cr. P. '22 Section 116; Cr. C. '12 Section 95; Cr. C. '02 Section 68; G. S. 2648;

R. S. 68; 1880 (17) 493; 1987 Act No. 49 Section 1, eff April 27, 1987.

SECTION 18-3-50. How bail shall be given.

Upon service of the notice the magistrate shall, on demand of the defendant, admit him to bail in such reasonable sum, and with good sureties, as the magistrate may require, with conditions:

(1) to appear at the court appealed to and at any subsequent term to which the case may be continued, if not previously surrendered, and so from term to term until the final decree, sentence or order of the court thereon;

(2) to abide such final sentence, order or decree and not depart without leave; and

(3) in the meantime to keep the peace and be of good behavior.

HISTORY: 1962 Code Section 7-105; 1952 Code Section 7-105; 1942 Code Section 1027; 1932 Code Section 1027; Cr. P. '22 Section 117; Cr. C. '12 Section 96; Cr. C. '02 Section 69; G. S. 2649; R. S. 69; 1880 (17) 493.

SECTION 18-3-60. Clerk shall enter case on motion calendar of court of common pleas.

The clerk of court, upon receipt of the case, shall place it upon the motion calendar of the court of common pleas.

HISTORY: 1962 Code Section 7-106; 1952 Code Section 7-106; 1942 Code Section 1028; 1932 Code Section 1028; Cr. P. '22 Section 118; Cr. C. '12 Section 97; Cr. C. '02 Section 70; G. S. 2650; R. S. 70; 1880 (17) 493; 1994 Act No. 520, Section 5, eff September 23, 1994.

SECTION 18-3-70. No examination of witnesses; action of court.

The appeal must be heard by the Court of Common Pleas upon the grounds of exceptions made and upon the papers required under this chapter, without the examination of witnesses in that court. And the court may either confirm the sentence appealed from, reverse or modify it, or grant a new trial, as to the court may seem meet and conformable to law.

HISTORY: 1962 Code Section 7-107; 1952 Code Section 7-107; 1942 Code Section 1029; 1932 Code Section 1029; Cr. P. '22 Section 119; Cr. C. '12 Section 98; Cr. C. '02 Section 71; G. S. 2651; R. S. 71; 1880 (17) 493; 1994 Act No. 520, Section 6, eff September 23, 1994.

CHAPTER 7 Appeals to Circuit and County Courts in Other Cases

ARTICLE 1 General Provisions

SECTION 18-7-10. Appeals from inferior courts; supersedeas.

When a judgment is rendered by a magistrates court, by the governing body of a county or by any other inferior court or jurisdiction, save the probate court, the appeal shall be to the circuit court of the county wherein the judgment was rendered and shall amount to a supersedeas if the party against whom judgment is rendered shall execute a good and sufficient bond with surety to pay the amount of the judgment and costs in the event that he fail to sustain such appeal. And in all cases in which such bond with surety shall be filed no executions shall issue until the termination of such appeal. Provided, that in any county in which a county court exists, appeals in such cases, except those from the probate courts and those that exceed the jurisdictional amounts of the respective county courts, shall be to the county court of the county.

HISTORY: 1962 Code Section 7-301; 1952 Code Section 7-301; 1942 Code Section 794; 1932 Code Section 794; Civ. P. '22 Section 659; Civ. P. '12 Section 397; Civ. P. '02 Section 358; 1870 (14) 369; 1887 (19) 832; 1937 (40) 81.

SECTION 18-7-20. When and how appeal shall be taken.

The appellant, within thirty days after written notice of judgment has been given him or his attorney by the magistrate, recorder, or judge of the municipal court, except when the judgment is announced at the trial in the presence of the appellant or his attorney then no written notice is necessary, shall serve a notice of appeal, stating the grounds upon which the appeal is founded. If the judgment is rendered upon process not personally served and the defendant did not appear, he has thirty days after personal notice of the judgment to serve the notice of appeal provided for in this section.

HISTORY: 1962 Code Section 7-302; 1952 Code Section 7-302; 1942 Code Section 795; 1932 Code Section 795; Civ. P. '22 Section 660; Civ. P. '12 Section 398; Civ. P. '02 Section 359; 1870 (14) 70; 1911 (27) 140; 1973 (58) 171; 1989 Act No. 20, Section 1, eff March 12, 1989.

SECTION 18-7-30. Contents of notice of appeal.

In the notice of appeal the appellant shall state in what particular or particulars he claims the judgment should have been more favorable to him. If he claims that the amount of judgment is less favorable to him than it should have been, he shall state what should have been its amount.

HISTORY: 1962 Code Section 7-303; 1952 Code Section 7-303; 1942 Code Section 809; 1932 Code Section 809; Civ. P. '22 Section 674; Civ. P. '12 Section 412; Civ. P. '02 Section 373; 1870 (14) 388; 1873 (15) 502 Section 20; 1880 (17) 297.

SECTION 18-7-60. Return; when and how made.

The court below shall thereupon, after ten days and within thirty days after service of the notice of appeal, make a return to the appellate court of the testimony, proceedings and judgment and file it in the appellate court.

HISTORY: 1962 Code Section 7-306; 1952 Code Section 7-306; 1942 Code Section 798; 1932 Code Section 798; Civ. P. '22 Section 663; Civ. P. '12 Section 401; Civ. P. '02 Section 362; 1870 (14) 377; 1880 (17) 306; 1972 (57) 2484.

SECTION 18-7-70. Return; how made if magistrate is out of office.

When a magistrate by whom a judgment appealed from was rendered shall have gone out of office before a return is ordered, he shall, nevertheless, make a return in the same manner and with the like effect as if he were still in office.

HISTORY: 1962 Code Section 7-307; 1952 Code Section 7-307; 1942 Code Section 799; 1932 Code Section 799; Civ. P. '22 Section 664; Civ. P. '12 Section 402; Civ. P. '02 Section 363; 1870 (14) 378.

SECTION 18-7-80. Return; further return when original is defective.

If the return be defective the appellate court may direct a further or amended return as often as may be necessary and may compel a compliance with its order. And the court shall always be deemed open for this purpose.

HISTORY: 1962 Code Section 7-308; 1952 Code Section 7-308; 1942 Code Section 800; 1932 Code Section 800; Civ. P. '22 Section 665; Civ. P. '12 Section 403; Civ. P. '02 Section 364; 1870 (14) 379; 1972 (57) 2484.

SECTION 18-7-90. Return; effect of dead, insane, or absent magistrate.

If a magistrate whose judgment is appealed from shall die, become insane or remove from the State before having made a return, the appellate court may examine witnesses on oath as to the facts and circumstances of the trial or judgment and determine the appeal as if the facts had been returned by the magistrate. If he shall have removed to another county within the State the appellate court may compel him to make the return as if he were still within the county where the judgment was rendered.

HISTORY: 1962 Code Section 7-309; 1952 Code Section 7-309; 1942 Code Section 801; 1932 Code Section 801; Civ. P. '22 Section 666; Civ. P. '12 Section 404; Civ. P. '02 Section 365; 1870 (14) 380.

SECTION 18-7-100. Offer to allow revision of judgment of magistrate.

Within fifteen days after the service of the notice of the appeal the respondent may serve upon the appellant and the magistrate an offer in writing to allow the judgment to be corrected in any of the particulars mentioned in the notice of appeal. The appellant may thereupon, and within five days thereafter, file with the magistrate a written acceptance of such offer, and in such case the magistrate shall thereupon make a minute of such acceptance in his docket and correct the judgment accordingly, and the judgment, so corrected, shall stand as his judgment and be enforced accordingly; and any execution which has been issued upon the judgment appealed from shall be amended by the magistrate to correspond with the amended judgment. If the offer be made and accepted by the appellant, the appellant shall recover all his disbursements on appeal and all his costs in the court below.

HISTORY: 1962 Code Section 7-310; 1952 Code Section 7-310; 1942 Code Section 809; 1932 Code Section 809; Civ. P. '22 Section 674; Civ. P. '12 Section 412; Civ. P. '02 Section 373; 1870 (14) 388; 1873 (15) 502; 1880 (17) 297.

SECTION 18-7-110. Offer to allow judgment on appeal.

In any appeal either party may, at any time before the trial, serve upon the opposite party an offer, in writing, to allow judgment to be taken against him for the sum or property or to the effect in such offer specified, and with or without costs as the offer shall specify. If the party receiving such offer accept it and give notice thereof in writing within ten days, he may file the return and offer, with an affidavit of service of notice of acceptance thereof, and judgment shall be entered thereon according to the offer. If the notice of acceptance be not given, the offer is to be deemed withdrawn and cannot be given in evidence.

HISTORY: 1962 Code Section 7-311; 1952 Code Section 7-311; 1942 Code Section 804; 1932 Code Section 804; Civ. P. '22 Section 669; Civ. P. '12 Section 407; Civ. P. '02 Section 368; 1870 (14) 383; 1873 (15) 502.

SECTION 18-7-130. Hearing of appeal.

The appeal shall be heard by the court upon all the papers in the case, including the testimony on the trial, which shall be taken down in writing and signed by the witnesses, and the grounds of exception made, without the examination of witnesses in court. The appeal shall be heard on the original papers and no copy thereof need be furnished for the use of the court.

HISTORY: 1962 Code Section 7-313; 1952 Code Section 7-313; 1942 Code Sections 794, 803; 1932 Code Sections 794, 803; Civ. P. '22 Sections 659, 668; Civ. P. '12 Sections 397, 406; Civ. P. '02 Sections 358, 367; 1870 (14) 369, 382; 1887 (19) 832; 1937 (40) 81.

SECTION 18-7-140. Powers of appellate court; amendment of pleadings.

The court shall have the same power over its own determinations, and shall render judgment thereon in the same manner, as the circuit court in actions pending therein, without trial by jury, and may allow either party to amend his pleadings upon such terms as shall be just.

HISTORY: 1962 Code Section 7-314; 1952 Code Section 7-314; 1942 Code Section 804; 1932 Code Section 804; Civ. P. '22 Section 669; Civ. P. '12 Section 407; Civ. P. '02 Section 368; 1870 (14) 383; 1873 (15) 502.

SECTION 18-7-150. New trial below when defendant did not appear.

If (a) the appellant failed to appear before the magistrate, (b) it is shown by the affidavits served by the appellant, or otherwise, that manifest injustice has been done and (c) the appellant satisfactorily excuses his default, the court may, in its discretion, set aside or suspend judgment and order a new trial before the same or any other magistrate in the same county at such time and place and on such terms as the court may deem proper. When a new trial shall be ordered before a magistrate the parties must appear before him according to the order of the court and the same proceedings must thereupon be had in the action as on the return of a summons personally served.

HISTORY: 1962 Code Section 7-315; 1952 Code Section 7-315; 1942 Code Section 804; 1932 Code Section 804; Civ. P. '22 Section 669; Civ. P. '12 Section 407; Civ. P. '02 Section 368; 1870 (14) 383; 1873 (15) 502.

SECTION 18-7-160. Motions for new trial in appellate court; other procedural rules.

Either party may move for a new trial in the appellate court on a case or exceptions, or otherwise, and such motion may be made before or after judgment has been entered; and the provisions of this code in relation to the proceedings, exceptions to the decisions of the court, making and settling cases and exceptions, motions for new trials and making up the judgment roll in the circuit court are hereby made applicable to all appeals brought up for trial as in this chapter provided.

HISTORY: 1962 Code Section 7-316; 1952 Code Section 7-316; 1942 Code Section 804; 1932 Code Section 804; Civ. P. '22 Section 669; Civ. P. '12 Section 407; Civ. P. '02 Section 368; 1870 (14) 383; 1873 (15) 502.

SECTION 18-7-170. Judgment on appeal.

Upon hearing the appeal the appellate court shall give judgment according to the justice of the case, without regard to technical errors and defects which do not affect the merits. In giving judgment the court may affirm or reverse the judgment of the court below, in whole or in part, as to any or all the parties and for errors of law or fact.

HISTORY: 1962 Code Section 7-317; 1952 Code Section 7-317; 1942 Code Section 804; 1932 Code Section 804; Civ. P. '22 Section 669; Civ. P. '12 Section 407; Civ. P. '02 Section 368; 1870 (14) 383; 1873 (15) 502.

SECTION 18-7-180. Judgment on appeal; appeals on errors in fact.

If the appeal is founded on an error in fact in the proceedings, not affecting the merits of the action and not within the knowledge of the magistrate, the court may determine the alleged error in fact on affidavits and may, in its discretion, inquire into and determine the alleged error upon examination of the witnesses. Every issue of fact so joined or brought upon an appeal shall be tried in the manner provided in Section 18-7-130.

HISTORY: 1962 Code Section 7-318; 1952 Code Section 7-318; 1942 Code Section 804; 1932 Code Section 804; Civ. P. '22 Section 669; Civ. P. '12 Section 407; Civ. P. '02 Section 368; 1870 (14) 383; 1873 (15) 502.

SECTION 18-7-190. Judgment on appeal; appeals on issue of law.

If the issue joined before the magistrate was an issue of law, the court shall render judgment thereon according to the law of the case; and if such judgment be against the pleadings of either party, an amendment of such pleading may be allowed on the same terms, and in like case, as pleadings in actions in the circuit court, and the court may thereupon require the opposite party to answer such amended pleading or join issue thereon, as the case may require, summarily. If upon an appeal in an issue of law the court should adjudge the pleading complained of to be valid, it shall, in like manner, require the opposite party summarily to answer such pleading or join issue thereon, as the case may require.

HISTORY: 1962 Code Section 7-319; 1952 Code Section 7-319; 1942 Code Section 804; 1932 Code Section 804; Civ. P. '22 Section 669; Civ. P. '12 Section 407; Civ. P. '02 Section 368; 1870 (14) 383; 1873 (15) 502.

SECTION 18-7-200. Procedure upon reversal of judgment already paid.

If the judgment below, or any part thereof, be paid or collected and the judgment be afterwards reversed, the appellate court shall order the amount paid or collected to be restored, with interest from the time of such payment or collection. The order may be obtained on proof of the facts made at or after the hearing, upon a previous notice of six days; and if the order shall be made before the judgment is entered, the amount may be included in the judgment.

HISTORY: 1962 Code Section 7-320; 1952 Code Section 7-320; 1942 Code Section 807; 1932 Code Section 807; Civ. P. '22 Section 672; Civ. P. '12 Section 410; Civ. P. '02 Section 371; 1870 (14) 386.

SECTION 18-7-210. Judgment roll.

To every judgment upon an appeal there shall be annexed the return on which it was heard, the notice of appeal and any offer, decision of the court, exceptions or case and all orders and papers in any way involving the merits and necessarily affecting the judgment, all of which shall be filed with the clerk of the court and shall constitute the judgment roll.

HISTORY: 1962 Code Section 7-321; 1952 Code Section 7-321; 1942 Code Section 805; 1932 Code Section 805; Civ. P. '22 Section 670; Civ. P. '12 Section 408; Civ. P. '02 Section 369; 1870 (14) 383.

SECTION 18-7-220. Costs on appeal.

Costs shall be allowed to the prevailing party in judgments rendered on appeal in all cases, with the exceptions and limitations stated in Sections 18-7-230 to 18-7-300.

HISTORY: 1962 Code Section 7-322; 1952 Code Section 7-322; 1942 Code Section 809; 1932 Code Section 809; Civ. P. '22 Section 674; Civ. P. '12 Section 412; Civ. P. '02 Section 373; 1870 (14) 388; 1873 (15) 502; 1880 (17) 297.

SECTION 18-7-230. Effect of failure to state error in judgment below on award of costs.

If in the notice of appeal the appellant shall not state in what particular or particulars he claims the judgment should have been more favorable to him, he shall not be entitled to costs unless the judgment appealed from shall be wholly reversed.

HISTORY: 1962 Code Section 7-323; 1952 Code Section 7-323; 1942 Code Section 809; 1932 Code Section 809; Civ. P. '22 Section 674; Civ. P. '12 Section 412; Civ. P. '02 Section 373; 1870 (14) 388; 1873 (15) 502; 1880 (17) 297.

SECTION 18-7-240. Costs when appellant gains less than ten dollars by appeal.

The appellant shall not recover costs unless the judgment appealed from shall be reversed on such appeal or be made more favorable to him to the amount of at least ten dollars.

HISTORY: 1962 Code Section 7-324; 1952 Code Section 7-324; 1942 Code Section 809; 1932 Code Section 809; Civ. P. '22 Section 674; Civ. P. '12 Section 412; Civ. P. '02 Section 373; 1870 (14) 388; 1873 (15) 502; 1880 (17) 297.

SECTION 18-7-250. Effect of rejection of offer under Section 18-7-100 on award of costs.

If an offer be made under the provisions of Section 18-7-100 and be not accepted and the judgment in the appellate court be not at least ten dollars more favorable to the appellant than the offer of the respondent, the respondent shall recover costs.

HISTORY: 1962 Code Section 7-325; 1952 Code Section 7-325; 1942 Code Section 809; 1932 Code Section 809; Civ. P. '22 Section 674; Civ. P. '12 Section 412; Civ. P. '02 Section 373; 1870 (14) 388; 1873 (15) 502; 1880 (17) 297.

SECTION 18-7-260. Effect of rejection of offer under Section 18-7-110 on award of costs.

If an offer be made under the provisions of Section 18-7-110 and be not accepted and if the party to whom such offer is made fail to obtain a judgment more favorable to him by at least ten dollars than that specified in the offer, then he shall not recover costs but must pay the other party's costs from the date of the service of the offer.

HISTORY: 1962 Code Section 7-326; 1952 Code Section 7-326; 1942 Code Sections 804, 809; 1932 Code Sections 804, 809; Civ. P. '22 Sections 669, 674; Civ. P. '12 Sections 407, 412; Civ. P. '02 Sections 368, 373; 1870 (14) 383; 1873 (15) 502 Section 20; 1880 (17) 297 Sections 2, 7.

SECTION 18-7-270. When award of costs is in discretion of court.

If the judgment appealed from be reversed in part and affirmed as to the residue, the amount of costs allowed to either party shall be such sum as the appellate court may award. If the judgment be reversed for an error of fact in the proceedings not affecting the merits, costs shall be in the discretion of the court.

HISTORY: 1962 Code Section 7-327; 1952 Code Section 7-327; 1942 Code Section 809; 1932 Code Section 809; Civ. P. '22 Section 674; Civ. P. '12 Section 412; Civ. P. '02 Section 373; 1870 (14) 388; 1873 (15) 502; 1880 (17) 297; 1972 (57) 2602.

SECTION 18-7-280. Award of costs when appeal is dismissed for want of prosecution.

If the appeal be dismissed for want of prosecution, as provided by Section 18-7-120, no costs shall be allowed to either party.

HISTORY: 1962 Code Section 7-328; 1952 Code Section 7-328; 1942 Code Section 809; 1932 Code Section 809; Civ. P. '22 Section 674; Civ. P. '12 Section 412; Civ. P. '02 Section 373; 1870 (14) 388; 1873 (15) 502; 1880 (17) 297.

SECTION 18-7-290. Award of costs to appellant shall include costs below.

Whenever costs are awarded to the appellant and when the judgment in the suit before the court below was against such appellant, he shall further be allowed to tax the costs incurred by him which he would have been entitled to recover in case the judgment below had been rendered in his favor.

HISTORY: 1962 Code Section 7-329; 1952 Code Section 7-329; 1942 Code Section 809; 1932 Code Section 809; Civ. P. '22 Section 674; Civ. P '12 Section 412; Civ. P. '02 Section 373; 1870 (14) 388; 1873 (15) 502; 1880 (17) 297.

SECTION 18-7-300. Setoff of costs against recovery.

If, upon an appeal, a recovery for any debt or damages be had by one party and costs be awarded to the other party, the court shall set off such costs against such debt or damages and render judgment for the balance.

HISTORY: 1962 Code Section 7-330; 1952 Code Section 7-330; 1942 Code Section 809; 1932 Code Section 809; Civ. P. '22 Section 674; Civ. P. '12 Section 412; Civ. P. '02 Section 373; 1870 (14) 388; 1873 (15) 502; 1880 (17) 297.

CHAPTER 9 Appeals to Supreme Court and Court of Appeals

SECTION 18-9-10. When appeal may be taken.

An appeal may be taken to the Supreme Court or the Court of Appeals in the cases mentioned in Sections 14-3-320 and 14-3-330. The procedure for taking an appeal is as provided by the South Carolina Appellate Court Rules.

HISTORY: 1962 Code Section 7-401; 1952 Code Section 7-401; 1942 Code Section 780; 1932 Code Section 780; Civ. P. '22 Section 645; Civ. P. '12 Section 383; Civ. P. '02 Section 344; 1870 (14) 358; 1991 Act No. 115, Section 3, eff June 5, 1991; 1999 Act No. 55, Section 26, eff June 1, 1999.

SECTION 18-9-20. Review of convictions of capital offenses.

The Supreme Court shall review each conviction of a capital offense by any court in this State.

HISTORY: 1962 Code Section 7-401.1; 1974 (58) 2361.

SECTION 18-9-30. Appeals in probate matters.

The Supreme Court and the Court of Appeals shall have jurisdiction of all questions of law arising in the course of the proceedings of the circuit court in probate matters in the same manner as provided by law in other cases.

HISTORY: 1962 Code Section 7-402; 1952 Code Section 7-402; 1942 Code Section 229; 1932 Code Section 229; Civ. P. '22 Section 186; Civ. P. '12 Section 62; Civ. P. '02 Section 56; 1870 (14) 56; 1999 Act No. 55, Section 27, eff June 1, 1999.

SECTION 18-9-40. Statement of questions of law and facts when questions certified.

When the circuit court shall render judgment upon a verdict taken, subject to the opinion of the court, the questions or conclusions of law together with a concise statement of the facts upon which they arose shall be prepared by and under the direction of the court, shall be filed with the judgment roll, and shall be considered a part of the judgment roll for the purposes of a review in the Supreme Court or the Court of Appeals.

HISTORY: 1962 Code Section 7-403; 1952 Code Section 7-403; 1942 Code Section 780; 1932 Code Section 780; Civ. P. '22 Section 645; Civ. P. '12 Section 383; Civ. P. '02 Section 344; 1870 (14) 358; 1999 Act No. 55, Section 28, eff June 1, 1999.

SECTION 18-9-50. Practice and proceedings on appeal from courts of general sessions.

The practice and proceedings in cases of appeal from the courts of general sessions shall conform to the practice and proceedings in cases of appeal from the courts of common pleas.

HISTORY: 1962 Code Section 7-404; 1952 Code Section 7-404; 1942 Code Section 1033; 1932 Code Section 1033; Cr. P. '22 Section 123; Cr. C. '12 Section 102; Cr. C. '02 Section 75; R. S. 74; 1884 (18) 737.

SECTION 18-9-130. Effect of notice of appeal on execution of judgment; sale of defendant's property; appeal in civil action involving signatory of Master Settlement Agreement.

(A)(1) A notice of appeal from a judgment directing the payment of money does not stay the execution of the judgment unless the presiding judge before whom the judgment was obtained grants a stay of execution. If the presiding judge grants a stay of execution and requires a bond or other surety to guarantee the payment of the judgment pending the appeal, the amount of the bond or other surety may not exceed the amount of the judgment or:

(a) twenty-five million dollars, whichever is less, for a business entity that employs more than fifty persons and has gross revenues exceeding five million dollars for the previous tax year; or

(b) one million dollars, whichever is less, for all other entities or individuals.

(2) A plaintiff may not enforce a sale of property after a notice of appeal is filed without giving an undertaking or bond to the defendant, with two good sureties, in double the appraised value of the property or double the amount of the judgment, conditioned to pay all damages the defendant may sustain by reason of the sale in case the judgment is reversed. The plaintiff in such a case may not proceed with a sale of defendant's property if the defendant enters into an undertaking, with good sureties, in double the appraised value of the property or the amount of the judgment, to pay the judgment with legal interest and all costs and damages the plaintiff may sustain by reason of the appeal or to produce the property levied on and submit to the sale if the judgment is confirmed.

(B)(1) The appeal of a judgment awarding relief in a civil action, under any legal theory, involving a signatory of the Master Settlement Agreement, as defined in Section 11-47-20(e), or a successor to or affiliate of a signatory to the agreement, automatically stays the execution of that judgment.

(2) The stay described in this subsection is effective upon the filing of the notice of appeal and during the entire course of appellate review of the judgment.

HISTORY: 1962 Code Section 7-412; 1952 Code Section 7-412; 1942 Code Section 782; 1932 Code Section 782; Civ. P. '22 Section 647; Civ. P. '12 Section 385; Civ. P. '02 Section 346; 1870 (14) 360; 1873 (15) 501; 2004 Act No. 216, Section 2, eff April 26, 2004; 2011 Act No. 52, Section 6, eff January 1, 2012.

Editor's Note

2004 Act No. 216, Section 3, provides as follows:

"This act takes effect upon approval by the Governor and applies to all cases pending on or filed on or after that date."

2011 Act No. 52, Section 7, provides as follows:

"SECTION 7. This act takes effect January 1, 2012, and applies to all actions that accrue on or after the effective date except the provisions of SECTION 3 do not apply to any matter pending on the effective date of this act."

SECTION 18-9-140. New undertaking in case sureties have become insolvent.

Whenever it shall be made satisfactorily to appear to the court that since the execution of an undertaking such as is mentioned in Section 18-9-130 the sureties have become insolvent, the court may by rule or order require the appellant to execute, file and serve a new undertaking meeting the requirements of that section and in case of failure to execute such undertaking within twenty days after the service of a copy of the rule or order requiring such new undertaking, the appeal may, on motion to the court, be dismissed with costs.

HISTORY: 1962 Code Section 7-413; 1952 Code Section 7-413; 1942 Code Section 783; 1932 Code Section 783; Civ. P. '22 Section 648; Civ. P. '12 Section 386; Civ. P. '02 Section 347; 1870 (14) 360.

SECTION 18-9-150. Deposit or surety when judgment requires delivery of documents or personalty.

If the judgment appealed from directs the assignment or delivery of documents or personal property, the execution of the judgment shall not be stayed by appeal unless the things required to be assigned or delivered be brought into court or placed in the custody of such officer or receiver as the court shall appoint or unless an undertaking be entered into on the part of the appellant, with at least two sureties and in such amount as the court or a judge thereof shall direct, to the effect that the appellant will obey the order of the appellate court upon the appeal.

HISTORY: 1962 Code Section 7-415; 1952 Code Section 7-415; 1942 Code Section 786; 1932 Code Section 786; Civ. P. '22 Section 651; Civ. P. '12 Section 389; Civ. P. '02 Section 350; 1870 (14) 361; 1999 Act No. 55, Section 29, eff June 1, 1999.

SECTION 18-9-160. Staying judgment to execute conveyance.

If the judgment appealed from directs the execution of a conveyance or other instrument, the execution of the judgment shall not be stayed by the appeal until the instrument shall have been executed and deposited with the clerk with whom the judgment is entered, to abide the judgment of the appellate court.

HISTORY: 1962 Code Section 7-416; 1952 Code Section 7-416; 1942 Code Section 787; 1932 Code Section 787; Civ. P. '22 Section 652; Civ. P. '12 Section 390; Civ. P. '02 Section 351; 1870 (14) 362; 1999 Act No. 55, Section 30, eff June 1, 1999.

SECTION 18-9-170. Staying judgment for sale or delivery of land.

If the judgment appealed from direct the sale or delivery of possession of real property, the execution of the judgment shall not be stayed unless a written undertaking be executed on the part of the appellant, with two sureties, to the effect that during the possession of such property by the appellant he will not commit or suffer to be committed any waste thereon and that if the judgment be affirmed he will pay the value of the use and occupation of the property from the time of the execution of the undertaking until the delivery of possession thereof pursuant to the judgment, not exceeding a sum to be fixed by a judge of the court by which judgment was rendered and which shall be specified in the undertaking. When the judgment directs the sale of land to satisfy a mortgage thereon or other lien, the undertaking shall provide that in case the judgment appealed from be affirmed and the land be finally sold for less than the judgment debt and costs then the appellant shall pay for any waste committed or suffered to be committed on the land and shall pay a reasonable rental value for the use and occupation of the land from the time of the execution of the undertaking to the time of the sale, but not exceeding the amount of such deficiency, which sum shall be duly entered as a payment on the judgment; and in case the land shall be unimproved land, then in any action or proceedings now pending or hereafter begun in any of the courts of this State the undertaking shall further provide for the payment by appellant, if the judgment be affirmed, of any taxes due at the time of the appeal or already paid by the mortgagee, or becoming due during the pendency of the appeal, and also for the payment by appellant of the interest on the debt falling due during the pendency of such appeal.

HISTORY: 1962 Code Section 7-417; 1952 Code Section 7-417; 1942 Code Section 788; 1932 Code Section 788; Civ. P. '22 Section 653; Civ. P. '12 Section 391; Civ. P. '02 Section 352; 1870 (14) 363; 1898 (22) 689; 1900 (23) 351.

SECTION 18-9-180. Stay of proceedings upon execution of bond or perfection of appeal.

Whenever the defendant executes the bond mentioned in Sections 18-9-130, 18-9-150 and 18-9-170 or the appeal is perfected as provided by Sections 18-9-150 or 18-9-160, it shall stay all further proceedings in the court below upon the judgment appealed from or upon the matter embraced therein; but the court below may proceed upon any other matter included in the action and not affected by the judgment appealed from.

HISTORY: 1962 Code Section 7-418; 1952 Code Section 7-418; 1942 Code Section 789; 1932 Code Section 789; Civ. P. '22 Section 654; Civ. P. '12 Section 392; Civ. P. '02 Section 353; 1870 (14) 364; 1873 (15) 501.

SECTION 18-9-190. Dispensing with or limiting security required.

The court below may, in its discretion, dispense with or limit the security required by Sections 18-9-130, 18-9-150 and 18-9-170, when the appellant is an executor, administrator, trustee or other person acting in another's right; and may also limit such security to the amount of less than fifty thousand dollars in the cases mentioned in Sections 18-9-150 and 18-9-170, when it would otherwise, according to those sections, exceed that sum.

HISTORY: 1962 Code Section 7-419; 1952 Code Section 7-419; 1942 Code Section 789; 1932 Code Section 789; Civ. P. '22 Section 654; Civ. P. '12 Section 392; Civ. P. '02 Section 353; 1870 (14) 364; 1873 (15) 501.

SECTION 18-9-200. Undertakings may be in one instrument or several; service on adverse party.

The undertakings prescribed by Sections 18-9-130, 18-9-140 and 18-9-170 may be in one instrument or several, at the option of the applicant, and a copy, including the names and residences of the sureties, must be served on the adverse party with notice of the appeal unless a deposit is made as provided in Section 15-1-250, and notice thereof given.

HISTORY: 1962 Code Section 7-420; 1952 Code Section 7-420; 1942 Code Section 790; 1932 Code Section 790; Civ. P. '22 Section 655; Civ. P. '12 Section 393; Civ. P. '02 Section 354; 1870 (14) 365; 1873 (15) 501.

SECTION 18-9-210. Justification by sureties; subsequent justification on new sureties.

An undertaking upon an appeal shall be of no effect, unless it be accompanied by the affidavit of the sureties that they are each worth double the amount specified therein. The respondent may, however, except to the sufficiency of the sureties within ten days after receipt of the notice of appeal; and unless they or other sureties justify before a judge or clerk of the court below, as prescribed by Sections 15-17-270 and 15-17-280, within ten days thereafter, the appeal shall be regarded as if no undertaking had been given. The justification shall be upon notice of not less than five days. No clerk shall take the justification of any surety or sureties in a case in which he may be interested or when either of the parties or such surety or sureties shall be connected with him by affinity or consanguinity within the sixth degree, and in all cases in which the clerk may have approved or disapproved of the sufficiency of a surety or sureties his action may be reviewed, on motion, after notice before a circuit judge. And in case at any time in any action a respondent shall be of opinion that the surety or sureties on any bond already approved are insufficient and shall make affidavit of the fact, setting out the grounds of such belief and serving a copy thereof upon appellant's attorney, then the sureties or other sureties shall justify anew thereon in the same manner and with the same effect as though such new justification were an original justification on such bond.

HISTORY: 1962 Code Section 7-421; 1952 Code Section 7-421; 1942 Code Section 791; 1932 Code Section 791; Civ. P. '22 Section 656; Civ. P. '12 Section 394; Civ. P. '02 Section 355; 1901 (23) 697.

SECTION 18-9-220. When notice of appeal stays proceedings below.

In cases not provided for in Sections 18-9-130 and 18-9-150 to 18-9-180, the notice of appeal shall stay proceedings in the court below upon the judgment appealed from, except that when it directs the sale of perishable property, the court below may order the property to be sold and the proceeds of the property to be deposited or invested in bonds of this State or of the United States, to abide the judgment of the appellate court.

HISTORY: 1962 Code Section 7-422; 1952 Code Section 7-422; 1942 Code Section 792; 1932 Code Section 792; Civ. P. '22 Section 657; Civ. P. '12 Section 395; Civ. P. '02 Section 356; 1887 (18) 837; 1889 (20) 355; 1999 Act No. 55, Section 31, eff June 1, 1999.

SECTION 18-9-230. Undertaking must be filed.

The undertaking must be filed with the clerk with whom the judgment or order appealed from was entered.

HISTORY: 1962 Code Section 7-423; 1952 Code Section 7-423; 1942 Code Section 793; 1932 Code Section 793; Civ. P. '22 Section 658; Civ. P. '12 Section 396; Civ. P. '02 Section 357; 1870 (14) 368.

SECTION 18-9-240. Security provisions apply to appeals in special proceedings.

The provisions of this chapter as to the security to be given upon appeals and as to the stay of proceedings shall apply to appeals taken under item (3) of Section 14-3-330.

HISTORY: 1962 Code Section 7-424; 1952 Code Section 7-424; 1942 Code Section 793; 1932 Code Section 793; Civ. P. '22 Section 658; Civ. P. '12 Section 396; Civ. P. '02 Section 357; 1870 (14) 368.

SECTION 18-9-270. Judgment of Supreme Court or Court of Appeals.

The Supreme Court or the Court of Appeals may reverse, affirm, or modify the judgment, decree, or order appealed from in whole or in part and as to any or all of the parties, and the judgment shall be remitted to the court below to be enforced according to law.

HISTORY: 1962 Code Section 7-427; 1952 Code Section 7-427; 1942 Code Section 27; 1932 Code Section 27; Civ. P. '22 Section 27; Civ. P. '12 Section 12; Civ. P. '02 Section 12; 1896 (22) 7; 1904 (24) 389; 1999 Act No. 55, Section 32, eff June 1, 1999.

SECTION 18-9-280. Written opinions required; memorandum opinions.

When a judgment or decree is reversed or affirmed by the Supreme Court every point made and distinctly stated in the cause and fairly arising upon the record of the case shall be considered and decided and the reason thereof shall be concisely and briefly stated in writing and preserved in the record of the case, except the Court may file memorandum opinions in unanimous decisions when the Court determines that a full written opinion would have no precedential value and any one or more of the following circumstances exists and is dispositive of a matter submitted to the Court for decision: (1) that a judgment of the trial court is based on findings of fact which are not clearly erroneous; (2) that the evidence of a jury verdict is not insufficient; (3) that the order of an administrative agency is supported by such quantum of evidence as prescribed by the statute or law under which judicial review is permitted; (4) that no error of law appears.

HISTORY: 1962 Code Section 7-428; 1952 Code Section 7-428; 1942 Code Section 27; 1932 Code Section 27; Civ. P. '22 Section 27; Civ. P. '12 Section 12; Civ. P. '02 Section 12; 1896 (22) 7; 1904 (24) 389; 1976 Act No. 530.

SECTION 18-9-290. Time for filing decisions.

The justices of the Supreme Court shall file their decisions within sixty days from the last day of the court at which the cases were heard.

HISTORY: 1962 Code Section 7-429; 1952 Code Section 7-429; 1942 Code Section 27; 1932 Code Section 27; Civ. P. '22 Section 27; Civ. P. '12 Section 12; Civ. P. '02 Section 12; 1896 (22) 7; 1904 (24) 389.

www.ingramcontent.com/pod-product-compliance
Lightning Source LLC
Chambersburg PA
CBHW080817220526
45466CB00011BB/3595